Breaking into Air

Breaking into Air

Birth Poems

Emily Wall

Book layout by Daniela Connor

Library of Congress Cataloging-in-Publication Data

Names: Wall, Emily, author.
Title: Breaking into air: birth poems / Emily Wall.
Description: First edition. | Pasadena: Boreal Books, [2022]
Identifiers: LCCN 2021042804 (print) | LCCN 2021042805 (ebook) | ISBN 9781597099233 (trade paperback) | ISBN 9781597099530 (epub)
Subjects: LCGFT: Poetry.
Classification: LCC PS3623.A35965 B74 2022 (print) | LCC PS3623.A35965 (ebook) | DDC 811/.6—dc23
LC record available at https://lccn.loc.gov/2021042804
LC ebook record available at https://lccn.loc.gov/2021042805

The National Endowment for the Arts, the Los Angeles County Arts Commission, the Ahmanson Foundation, the Dwight Stuart Youth Fund, the Max Factor Family Foundation, the Pasadena Tournament of Roses Foundation, the Pasadena Arts & Culture Commission and the City of Pasadena Cultural Affairs Division, the City of Los Angeles Department of Cultural Affairs, the Audrey & Sydney Irmas Charitable Foundation, the Meta & George Rosenberg Foundation, the Albert and Elaine Borchard Foundation, the Adams Family Foundation, Amazon Literary Partnership, the Sam Francis Foundation, and the Mara W. Breech Foundation partially support Red Hen Press.

First Edition
Published by Boreal Books
An imprint of Red Hen Press
www.borealbooks.org
www.redhen.org

Acknowledgments

My thanks to the following journals in which these poems first appeared, sometimes in different form.

Adanna: "Do Not Look at a Lunar Eclipse," "In the Birthing Tub, Afterwards"; *Alaska Quarterly Review*: "Shaawatke'é's Birth"; *Christianity and Literature*: "Mary's Homebirth, Bethlehem"; *Evening Street Review*: "Catching Babies: Haiku"; *Flame*: "Mary as Midwife, Nazareth," "Mary's Homebirth, Bethlehem," "Mary's Belly, Savta's House"; *Literary Mama*: "Hazel's Birth"; *Minerva Rising*: "Saki's Birth"; *Naugatuck Review* and *Best Indie Lit New England*, vol. ii: "Heart Lottery"; *Prairie Schooner*: "Samantha's Births"; *Room*: "All You Have to Do Is Open"; and *WomenArts Quarterly*: "Henry's Birth."

I am also deeply grateful to the mothers and fathers who shared their birth stories for this project: Shayna Rowher, Sarah Jaquette Ray, X'unei Lance and Miriah Káalaa Twitchell, Stephanie and Wendy Perry, Sharra Liptack, Sharon and Fred Wall, Andrew and Lisa Uzunoe, Wendy Erd, Rachel Gladhart, Susan Koester, Summer Koester, and Reverend Melissa Engel. Thanks to everyone who participated in the Facebook poll asking what a fetal heartbeat sounds like. Special thanks to the three Juneau doctors who shared stories; they asked to remain anonymous to protect the confidentiality of their patients and children.

Thanks also to James Englehardt, Rod Landis, and Taylor McKenna who shared their good editing advice. Special thanks to Peggy Shumaker whose generosity and guidance helped finish this book.

Research for the Mary triptych came from the book *Mary: A Flesh-and-Blood Biography of the Virgin Mother* by Lesley Hazleton.

This project is funded in part by the Juneau Arts and Humanities Council and the City and Borough of Juneau.

For AnnaCaroline, Helen Josephine, and Lucy Louisa
For Corey, who helped me birth these girls
For Debi Ballum and the OB nurses at Bartlett Regional Hospital
And for Dr. Don Schneider, who helped birth all three girls

This book is also for Shawnya, Jonathan, Saki, and Noah. We miss you.

CONTENTS

What Does a Fetal Heartbeat Sound Like?

—a found poem

Like feet running on wet sand.

Like horses
galloping horses
like a hummingbird
a hundred hummingbirds in a snowstorm.

Like a country music station picked up

like being underwater and fish
listening to our kicking
like an off-balance washing machine
like a Hula-Hoop, spinning.

Like a double
double heartbeat one fast
one slow

like the sound of God
like horses, always.

Like wind blowing (wish wish)
like a Japanese wooden flute
like a window, opening

like blood pumping
to muscles, to fingers,
to toes, to lungs and to skin.

Like horses
like feet running on wet sand,
like hummingbirds.

Like hope.

Breaking into Air

Henry's Birth

for Shayna

Henry rests upon the floor of the world
as you rock, and open, and sing
into a feral place, where you hold

onto your kitchen counter, touch the cold
blue tiles, small ponds of quiet, that will bring
Henry, resting upon the floor of the world.

Your body begins to fill, to flood
blood, sweat, urine. You begin slipping
into a feral place, where you hold

your goodbyes. Everyone else waits for hello
while you feel him leave the cradle of your being,
Henry, resting, upon the floor of the world.

And then it's time to let go. The midwife has told
you this moment would come, yet you linger
in that feral place, where you hold

your hands in the rich loam of birth, feel the bold
cracking of your body, a rock deep and sweet
as Henry, resting upon the floor of the world,
in this feral place, where you hold and hold and hold.

It begins with loss. Sleeping on the red sofa, I wake, feel this breaking, this spilling. A gush, a trickle, a slow wave roar.

Samantha's Births

for Stephanie and Wendy

Birth One

Samantha,
you touched down in a bottle
the color of stars

at the Spokane cryobank
on a silvery day, scales
of soft rain coming down.

The man handed
your cradle to me
and I held you first

the sleek tail
that would become your backbone
and your other momma

held me, touched the smallest
sliver of you. We strapped this
swimming, shimmering you

    strong and strong

into a car seat, for the drive
home.

Birth Two

You were conceived
in quiet
on an afternoon
of hollow bones, and I
dreamed later of a beach
full of gull feathers
and how I filled
my hands with them, trying to find
the one feather
that would become
your face.

Birth Three

I drank a sea-full
of water, floated
in a warm bath,
your momma by my side

light scaling the windows
of the hospital room

as you swam and turned
and fishtailed through
me as I watched

your coming
in a mirror, with each push

          strong and strong

watched your sleek head
turning coming turning
as you swam into light

into a room where your momma
held the skin gates open
and your NaNa held the heartbeat

machine, pressed to belly between
contractions, and everyone listened
to the sound of your name

chanted over and over
one hundred forty beats a minute

strong and strong

until you were ready. You pulled
your soft fins out of the socket
of me, and let go

of that deep ocean
swam into the sound of your heartbeat
into the sound of your momma

calling your name, my name
your NaNa breathing
with your mommas, with your midwife

easing your dark head
into the light and then your clean
fish body slipped up onto my chest

and your momma put her
hands on your head
holding
as much of you as she could
and you rested

on the soft sand dunes
of your mothers

strong and strong

our momma-talk
drying you. Our hands
opening, finally,
          your own silver wings.

Mary as Midwife, Nazareth

There is a curve
of moon although it's still

deepest night, as it usually
is, when a boy comes running.

His calling wakes Savta and me.
Will we help?

We enter the house and a fire
is already burning, the men already

on the roof. Good. Savta
places the birth stone. I mix

the herbs with wine
and tip it to her lips. This almost

mother takes it gratefully, swallows
the bitter help.

Savta sits on the stone between
her legs. The woman's sisters

squat beside her
one for each heavy thigh.

We talk the baby out.
We quietly share a glance

that it's a girl. Then we call to
the placenta. *Come, sister.*

She needs to arrive now
or the mother will die, and we call

into the night as the exhausted
mother does this last, hard

work, the birthing of the baby's
small room. The final emptying

of her womb. We do our work well
and then Savta and I eat a few bites

of bread, breathe in the smell of blood
and new skin. We walk home

in the final hours of darkness, under
that faint curve of moon. *Come, sister.*

Do Not Look at a Lunar Eclipse

—a found poem

Do not place scissors in your bed
or the baby will have a cleft palate.

Put a paste of ginger tea and cocoa butter
on your belly, to avoid stretch marks;
dress warmly, always, for this hot condition.

Never braid your hair, wear rings
or necklaces
or the umbilical cord will choke him.

Don't let anything ugly be seen,
don't criticize anyone
or the baby will be disagreeable.

Don't cry out during labor,
don't attract evil spirits.

Slip a necklace around her neck
before the cord is cut
tethering her to this world.

No drinking hot coffee,
no eating hot chilies
or baby may get rashes.

Eat sesame soup, cream,
coconut milk, ginger tea
to make sweet milk.

When the baby is coming, go
into the *aanigutyak*. After birth, go
into the tent prepared with steam and lemongrass

stay inside after the baby is born, wrap him
in socks and blankets, let no rain fall on him
take no baths.

Take the placenta and plant
it under a fruit tree
or cut it up and bury it, away from animals,

bury the umbilical cord nearby
so the child will always come home.
Eat only vegetables and rice.
Eat lots of moose, seal, caribou.

Let the priest baptize her, the shaman
name her, let the monk place the woven band
on her wrist. Let the women bless her.

Let the women bless her.

I walk the hospital halls, up and down in a double gown, borrowed socks, thick and warm. At one end, a photo collage of babies, at the other end, pain. I keep walking back into pain, down into pain, with little pauses to breathe. A Oaxacan woman giving birth becomes a warrior, climbs down a ladder into the underworld. She looks for the spirit holding her child, then fights him. Would she pause, look up at everyone above, now just small points against the sky?

Focal Point

Out the hospital window:
a ridge of muscled rock

an anchored spruce,
low clouds caught

in thick branches.
Somewhere higher

on the mountain, deer
sleep, or eat soft leaves.

Soon another
contraction will come.

Now I am afraid of them,
of the screams they pull from me,

organized me, quiet me, who
prefers to sit on the floor at a party

who prefers to be home
with a book, watching mist

rise from water. It will be
only seconds now, before I

lose control. I watch the way
the spruce branches catch

and hold, catch and hold,
as the mist moves through.

Maybe this time.

That ridge
of muscled rock.

That anchored spruce.
Those arms, full of water.

All You Have to Do Is Open

You polish your belly with cream,
   henna vines on its sleek curve
      let strangers Buddha rub it.

In birth class they tell you
   your body was made for this. They tell you
      your mother was strapped down and drugged.

You are capable of doing so much more:
   of squatting, of controlling your contractions
      of talking to your baby, guiding her out.

Picture your cervix opening, opening
   they tell you, and you see mandalas everywhere—
      the stone labyrinth

at the Shrine of St. Thérèse spiraling inward
   taking you closer and closer
      to the quiet mind, the open heart.

But then it begins, and you discover you are not
   made for this. A midwife shakes her head, retracts
      her hands. Another says *you're not allowing yourself to open.*

As if you were keeping your body
   in pain, as if you were locked
      against the arrival of your child. *Just let go, just breathe*

they say, and instead you scream, wonder what's wrong
   with you. Finally, your beautiful belly is cracked
      open like a stubborn egg, as you lie

on the table, returned to the rooms
        of halogen lights, the rooms of knives
                and needles in the spine.

And then comes the part where you don't have enough
        milk, where the hormones aren't flooding (is it your fault?
                is it the drugs?). The part where you hold the baby

and love her, a little, but not enough, not yet.
        Where you face the failure of your cervix,
                the failure of your breathing, or maybe

it's the fault of the midwife, the doctor who just wanted to go home
        and you try to get out of your fucked up mind
                enough to just hold the baby.

To mold this moment into what you thought
        it would be, into what everyone expects
                except the midnight shift nurse, who comes in

when they've all left, who checks your wound, who lets her hand linger
        on your misshapen belly. Who simply says
                You are her mother. You are her mother

and *nothing in this world is perfect.*
        And for a moment she looks like a visionary
                in her green scrubs.

Remember this, you tell yourself,
        This is what I will tell my daughter someday.

I lower the stone of myself into the water. I want to float, I want to sink. I want to climb out of everything but my husband's voice, telling me the story of our thousand-mile sail. Listen. I see our white dinghy on a rocky beach in a small cove, water lapping at its stern. I see each small stone. Small-round-hard. I imagine picking one up, the casual power my hands once had. I can taste the rain-smell of this rock. I put it in my mouth, suck its smooth edges.
Small, round, hard.

Hazel's Birth

for Sarah

I am under a crush of ice
a sheet of needles over the water of my body

my hands pressed against it, looking up
at everyone else

looking down at me. Yes,
their hands are pressed to the ice, trying

to hold my own, but they are breathing
air, and I, I am looking for the next

breathing hole, the place where I can rise
and take a mouthful of air.

This is day three. I sit in the bed, pushing,
I sit in the bath, pushing, I let

the midwife massage my cervix, pushing.
She breaks my waters, that beautiful pillow

between me and more pain, that cradle for my
daughter's head that I've protected for months

now, and I'm pushing again, willing with every
muscle for the word *progress*. That's the only word

that matters now. Not, *do it for your baby*
(fuck you!), not *visualize your baby* just

look at me, look at my face, and tell me:
I'm making progress.

I feel a warm hand on my face
and there is a doctor,

pushing the hair out of my eyes
with such tenderness. This woman

is here, she is pulling me
from beneath the ice.

Drugs in my spine, an operating table,
a tent to block my body from myself—

the litany of nightmares I have worked
so hard to avoid.

She is taking my hand, pulling me out,
and as I rise, I remember *Hazel*.

That beautiful name is sweetness,
melting on my tongue, and I swallow

great breaths of air, grateful
to be back in my body.

Kiss your daughter says the doctor,
and there she is, bloody, beautiful.

She wipes off a spot
for my lips, but I don't care

I want to inhale this baby whole.
I press my face

to hers, breathe her in,
beautiful, beautiful.

I touch her hair, thick as the midwife
had promised, connecting

that womb life with this person
next to me. Sweet girl, delicious girl.

Finally, Hazel. Finally, me.
Floating, for a while, before

I'm flooded with
the what ifs and the if onlys

and everyone else's
feelings, which just don't matter.

This is about me, and Hazel,
stepping out of that dark lake,

stepping onto the shore,
and learning how to breathe.

Then my hips unhinge, I am on my knees, the doctor says we have a problem he holds my hand gently but he talks so slowly they all speak so carefully don't they realize stop telling me to breathe, maybe it's all they have to give they know it's not enough it's not any kind of gift but they can't stand there watching this, he finally suggests the needle and I am a thousand years past ready, a lifetime beyond my birth plan this isn't birth anymore this isn't even a baby this is just breaking this is just not-breathing.

This Birth Instead

for Wendy

I can see you now, diving on the gorgeous reef
of sex with your boyfriend, blue sheets a tissue
of water, misted by your bodies, and the exotic

salts of love. Years later, you dream an exotic
fish growing in your belly, but the doctor says a reef
has formed in your ocean, a twist of scar tissue

between sea and shore. Your womb a fragile tissue
dissolving. So you travel with your husband to exotic
places. You work for peace. Birth instead a colorful reef

of prayer flags. I see you now, touching those exotic tissues, your reef of hope.

Shaawatke'é's Birth

for Ḵáalaa Miriah Twitchell

x'óol' yáx̱ yatee.[1]

Whirlpool.

ax̱ yádi
ax̱ yádi

i eegáa ḵuwtuwashée.
i eegáa ḵuwtuwashée.[2]

In this house of chaos—your sister learning
language, your mother sleeping, sleeping in the back room

my father leaving, my mother arriving, phone ringing,
everyone needing a bath, the long hours of light

too bright. Listen: sometimes late, late at night
I place my hands on your mother's belly

place my hands on your skin house
and what my fingers see is your ears,

small clamshells, listening listening to the summer
rain of Lingít, the pattern of us, tapping into you.

How shall I stack these words?
What is the first word to give you?

---

1 it's chaotic, like a whirlpool

2 my child.
  my child.

  we were looking for you.
  we were looking for you.

wéidu i tláa,
i tláa áwé.

x̱át áyá, i éesh.
gunalchéesh.
gunalchéesh.[3]

Then comes that long summer night
when we know you are coming.

Your rich river breaks on the rock
in the backyard, the rock under the cedar tree

and you are coming quickly quickly
in the birthing room.

And now your tongue is a salmon
swimming downstream, heading

for the ocean of sound, ready to take your first swallow
of salt water, ready to taste your first vowels

rain on ocean, and your ear and tongue, coming now
and pain is here too, and your mother in pain.

wáang̲aneens
tlax̱ lidzee áyá yá k̲ustí,

---

3 there is your mother.
  that is your mother.

me, i am your father.
thank you.
thank you.

ch'a haa kát uwagút.

haa yoo x̱'atángi yaa nanáan

i een áyá ḵu.aa,
kei gux̱latseen.
kei gux̱latseen:

haa Lingítx̱ sateeyí.[4]

And what I know to do is this
and what I know to do is this:

I ask that we turn down the lights
I ask that no one speak. Your first

sound above water will be the language
of black feathers, the language of flight.

I ease into the water, feel your head,
feel its turning until a furled ear emerges

and another, your body coming
swimming into the sound, rising into the sound

---

4 sometimes
this life is so difficult,
it has come upon us.

our language is dying.

but with you, though,
it will get stronger.
it will get stronger:

our Lingít identity

of my voice. I hold the air around you.
I blow softly into your ear, to open its listening:

> *woosh tudzix̱án*
> *haa yoo x̱'atángi een*
>
> *woosh tudzix̱án*
> *haa yoo x̱'atángi een.*[5]

We love each other
and this is your language

we love you in this language
we love you and this is you

sliding wetly into my hands,
your seal-soft mouth opening

and you have the most beautiful
tongue I've ever seen. Strong organ

at the center of the world, strong
voice, at the center of my world.

> *gunalchéesh, gunalchéesh*
> *yéi áwé.*[6]

---

5 we love each other
with our language

we love each other
with our language

6 thank you, thank you
that is how it is.

Mary's Belly, Savta's House

Midday and the heat
is intense. I spend my hours

now in the courtyard,
grinding herbs, pounding wheat,

learning to cook. Growing
a belly means it is time to learn

to feed others. Savta teaches
me, watches over me. *Like this,*

she says, folding the dough
under my hands. *Like this.*

When it's too hot
we go in and she pulls

out a pot of olive oil.
I lie down. This is my favorite

part of the day. She rubs circles
of oil over my belly, easing the dry

skin. I can feel her talking
to the baby with her hands.

*Before they are born, this is the way
we talk to them.* She says

I will have a boy. *He will hear
your hands, speaking to him. You must*

talk to him, every day. I lie
on the cool floor, feel the heat

of the oil seep into my skin. It feels
so good, just to rest, for a minute.

I know you are thinking: can she really
be carrying the son of Yahweh?

Can she really be a virgin? Did she really
see an angel?

These are beautiful questions.
I dip one finger in the oil on my belly

lift it, let it shine in the slant
of light from the open door.

I am beautiful too, just now.
I touch my belly.

Hush now. I'm talking
to my boy.

This is me, sleeping. Enormous, in this soft bed. All around me, is sleeping. The doctor has gone off to his small, quiet room. My husband sleeps in the chair. Two nurses are awake, talking quietly. I wrap myself in white sheets, drift away from that island of pain, listen to the wind hush me along. I don't point my little sloop. I don't look back.

Saki's Birth

for my sister Lisa

We lost Saki
after just two months
in her mama's belly.

> At least they have
> Jubei, everyone said.

Why do we say she's lost?

> This mother
> knows where she is—

there, just under the skin
there, curled inside this bone house.

Why would another child
mean less grief?

> Yes, someone to put her arms around.
> Someone to distract her with breakfast.

But that space below the ribs remains
an empty house
even if later babies come along.

She will always have to walk past those windows,
those closed shutters. She will always want to sweep
that small yard with her hand.

Heart Lottery

After her first son was born
      with a heart defect, she insisted
on testing in the second pregnancy.
      Her doctor said *no,*
her doctor said, *better chance of winning the lottery than a second defect*
      her doctor said *insurance.*
But she insisted: order the test. I'll pay for it.
      I'll fly to Seattle. I'll be the foolish one.
And so she did—lying on the crinkly, vinyl bed
      in the quiet room, ultrasound machine humming
like nervous thoughts over her head, the tech
      bored and humming too, and then—there it was—
the *winning-the-lottery-second-defect.*
      They stared at the little thumping heart
opening and closing the wrong way. They would do surgery
      the day after he was born.
If you would have had this baby in Ketchikan,
      the heart specialist told her, *he would have died.*
Which she had known, and hadn't known.
      She had simply scratched her thumb against her own fearful heart,
hoping for the one break she needed.

I hear them calling me back, telling me it's time to push. A nurse steps to my side, and I see her own growing belly. And on the other side, my husband, who begins to count for me, as I row back to shore. I row and row and row and row.

On Call

The doctor is at the gym
the nurse tells me, while I labor,

contractions fisting my body.
She doesn't come. And doesn't come.

Then when she finally does, she's thin, glowing,
says *you're doing great*. I hate her.

Then a shift change, and another doctor
arrives as I reach ten centimeters.

She holds my ankles, has complicated
instructions for me, for pushing.

But it's my doctor I am waiting for.
The one who has spent years studying

my body, who walked beside me all that long night
with my first, difficult birth.

So I wait, even though everyone says *push*.
I know the on-call rules, I've been warned, but still, I wait. Breathe. Wait.

And then he swings through the door, shirt un-tucked,
smiling, hands spread wide

and I feel my whole body unfist.

He puts his hands on my knees, says
I'm here. We're ready. Let's push.

I push for a lifetime, for ten thousand years. I push for the time it takes each petal on a cherry tree to blossom. I know there is a baby, I know she's coming, but this knowledge is far-off—like knowing the moon creates tides. What I know right now is volcanoes and blisters on my palms, and a tired pregnant nurse holding me up, and so much water to move through yet. What I know right now is pain, and tearing, and stuck.

Ryan's Birth

for Rachel

Scientific intervention
miscarriages
didn't believe
odds against us
5 percent successful
last egg
take a chance.

Not Braxton Hicks
every six to eight minutes
cervix unaware
gestational diabetes
thirty-five weeks
can't birth in Juneau.

4:00 a.m.
breaking water
whirlwind
children home alone
medevac in twenty minutes
texting husband: *come back*
ambulance
doctor walking us
to plane
beautiful fall morning.

Medevac nurses
fetal heart tones
2 cm
plane fascinating.

Corner room OB unit
Swedish, Seattle
6–7 cm
boost lungs
steroids, monitors
maternal fetal medicine
little intervention
pasta, carbohydrates
hypnobirthing meditations.

Can't feel cervix
OB attending
residents
chorus commands.
Husband whispers.
twenty minutes pushing
cut
bruised
broken capillaries
low blood sugar
baby, whisked away.

NICU team
lung retractions
working too hard
to breathe
CPAP machine
naked
vital sign monitors
IV in hand, mound of tape
tubes in face.

Every twelve hours
skin to skin
nurses drop everything
when we ask
skin to skin
no stroking, overly stimulating
too cold too stressed
skin to skin
jaundice lights
we learn hand hugs.

Children shuttled to friends
insurance questions, postpartum hormones
husband
brings food
cleans breast pump
treks to NICU, middle of the night
carrying
drops of colostrum.

NICU bedside vigil
sleeping in chair
in postpartum room
in NICU parent room
in hotel bed
back to hospital.

Finally
decreased oxygen needs
feeding tube out
IV discontinued
up to us now.

Baby named
Ryan
longer, rounder
two weeks old, coming home
baby on the ferry,
this sweet boy
breathing.

Catching Babies: Haiku

for the Juneau doctors, who shared these stories

First, out came a fist.
Now I'm not just doctor
but her first handhold.

She is just fifteen
delivers on hallway floor
asks: where's the TV?

Mom sits on dad's lap
who sits on top of toilet.
Baby drops in my hands.

The first baby I
delivered, an accident:
just me in the room.

Obese twelve-year-old
no idea a baby
is crowning. Right now.

I kneel between legs
waiting. The parents both watch
a porn film on TV.

Mom on drugs, baby
dead, cord dangling. In dark
room, I hold him close.

Not on call but I
came, in my camping gear, stayed
for twenty-five hours.

Young mom claps her hands
at ten centimeters, says:
let's go people!

Emergency room
gunshot wound, pregnant mother.
My first dead baby.

From the birth center
she came screaming, defeated
already hating me.

I meet the airplane
on the tarmac, girl from Haines,
to say: you're safe now.

*So my doctor pulls lists of ideas from his flannel sleeves, tricks to get us unstuck.
I flip my body, I focus my mind, we push differently, we take needles out, we try
new instruments. Now even I am ready to be cut open, but he keeps working.
He's still in his camping gear, he didn't leave, and that flannel shirt, that baseball
cap, help. I can see Echo Cove, Bridget Cove, all the places of wet rock and cedar.
I picture the meditation circle at the Shrine of St. Thérèse, walking through the
labyrinth chanting to my cervix: open open unspool uncurl. I see myself climbing
back up the ladder, this one made of spruce needles. I see a surf scoter just off the
beach, on a stormy day. I see her riding the storm, riding the waves, I see her open
her wings. I see her begin to lift.*

Teagan's Birth

for Sue and Summer

You open the door and your daughter is breathing
through a contraction, hands on knees
the toddler twirling around her, *Mama Mama*
husband wrestling with the birthing tub.

You already know what to do: what shoes
to slip on your grandson, which coat is right
for the playground, how to buckle the car seat
without pinching, how to sing, how to distract.

You know how to tire a boy out, how to
push him on the swings until your arms ache,
just how long to wait before worrying
when he's not in your line of sight.

You sit in an empty swing, imagine your daughter
breathing, walking, rocking in the tub,
midwife there, urging her to sip water.
She will light candles, remind Summer she is *home*

exactly where she wants to be.
You remember birthing her in your own home
in the cabin on the beach, wind whipping the waves
that day. How you talked Summer out

surprised that you knew just what to do.
Your two midwives, illegal back then, knelt
at your side, your husband, your mother
stroked your palms.

This midwife will know exactly where
to put her hands. Summer will know when to turn,

when to kneel, when to ask for what she needs.
She will know how to talk her daughter out.

And you know when it's time to tell your grandson
it's time to go. Is it just a feeling you hold
in your own belly? You lift him into the car seat
and he falls asleep, as you knew he would.

Back at the house you lift the latch
on the door, child on your shoulder snoring.
You enter the room and see
your granddaughter, crowning.

Of course you knew when to come.
Of course she knows how to push, how to breathe.
How to reach down and pull her daughter up,
up, into the light.

Mary's Homebirth, Bethlehem

—a haiku

What she does have is
a stone, perfect for beating
the floor. Her mantra.

Stone. Stone. No breaking
no blood. Just opening
just opening.

Between contractions
in this ridiculous place
of straw and stone walls

she admires the
stone, its perfect symmetry
its ungentle beauty.

Stone. Stone. No breaking
no blood. Just opening
just opening.

And later, baby
beside her, she is glad for
the animal warmth

the slow ease with which
they witnessed her bloody birth
calm and calmer still.

But it is the stone
she loves, will not put down.
The stone she slips

into her pocket.
Small, hard womb. Unbreakable
body.

Our First Sleep

for Ellie Jo, six hours old

I wake every three hours
to your small arm waving
in the dark.

Your fingers rake the air
testing the waters, to see if
I am still near.

A little snore floats past,
the leaves of a dream,
a current of cold.

I reach out and pluck
you into the boat
of me, curve around you,

fill your mouth
with my warm breast.
Listen to you draw me in.

All around us the cold night
currents and eddies,
against the timbers of our sleep

and I can imagine it will be this easy
to keep you this close. This safe
above the world's deep waters.

And then, when I realize why mothers die in childbirth, when I am limp and wet in the bed, her head drops down. We see, finally, the dark sky of her hair. My doctor, my husband, these two men, gently put their hands on us, begin to guide her out. I am birthing a fiery star. I feel each shoulder leave me, her rounded belly, the rays of her legs, each shining foot. And before I can take the next breath she is on my belly. They are rubbing her, she isn't crying, and now my whole being is focused on warmth and breath. I push heat from my skin to hers, and breathe breathe, to get her into the rhythm. This isn't about miracles or doctors or God or motherhood or hope. It's just me warming her body, teaching her to breathe, watching for the slow blush of pink to spread from face, to belly, to those cool, gray feet.

Waiting for Sophia

for Reverend Melissa

You send me a note tonight: your labor has begun.
You light candles, one for each of the women praying for you.
You surround yourself with light, with flame, with breath.
I hold my hands to my belly, to the dark sky, holding you.

You light candles, one for each of the women praying for you.
Each Sunday, you get up, with your big belly, and bless us.
I hold my hands to my belly, to the dark sky, holding you.
You break bread, you ring the singing bowl, you create quiet.

Each Sunday, you get up, with your big belly, and bless us.
You invite the children up to share their thoughts on God.
You break bread, you ring the singing bowl, you create a quiet
space for their voices to be heard, all these little girls.

You invite the children up to share their thoughts on God.
They touch your belly, ask about Mary and Joseph, about giving birth
and you let their voices be heard, all these little girls.
You tell them, Sophia means wisdom.

They touch your belly, ask about Mary and Joseph, about giving birth.
Now six days before Christmas, I light my Virgin Mary votive.
You tell them, Sophia means wisdom.
I close my eyes, and breathe with you: *come, Sophia. Come, sister.*

Now six days before Christmas, I light my Virgin Mary votive.
My girls and I stand in a circle and pray for you, now twenty hours in.
I close my eyes and breathe with you. *Come Sophia. Come Sister.*
And all across town, the women you teach stay awake, wait.

My girls and I stand in a circle and pray for you, now twenty hours in.
You sent me a note tonight to tell me your labor had begun.

All across town, the women you teach stay awake, wait.
You are surrounded now by our light, by our flame. By our blessing breath.

But then the nurses rubbing the baby exchange a look and lift her away, rush her across the room. I panic, stop breathing, feel another strong contraction, try to speak, but have lost my voice. The doctor starts a mantra for me, saying it's-okay-she's-okay over and over. She isn't breathing as well as they want, they call a pediatrician, I can't see the baby, and I am having contractions again, the placenta trying to birth itself, and I can't stay in this bed, in this body, in this more pushing. It's-okay-she's-okay. I start to shake, can't control the spasms of cold. A nurse brings me a heated blanket, wraps me tightly. Then brings me another. You're-okay. She's-okay.

Shawnya Hope's Birth

for Fred and Sharon

He shaved and showered. We thought there was time. *Keep trying.*

     How many children do you have?

Letdown and milk is what's coming, now. A pink sweater.

          In the hallway, on the gurney, her heartbeat strong. I hear it.

That long night alone
in the hospital
I feel her move around this room
of leaves I have made, red maples
pressed together, patterned with drops
of soft rain. She is sleeping in the
cradle of me, waking to feed,
maybe dreaming.
Today will be her birthday. The day after
                 her older sister's. I'm making a chocolate cake.

The doctor is sleeping at home. Weeks ago he studied the blood
on his gloved hand,
was unsure how to say   *I don't know what to say.*

     When we go to Willow River in a few weeks
          I'll let the kids splash around
     I'll cover this baby with my red umbrella.
          I'll dig a little shallow in the sand
     so she will be warm.

How many children do you have?
My mother. My sister.

Fred, alone at the funeral home. On the way home from the hospital we choose a pink sweater.
Washable wool.

My legs in stirrups
alone in the delivery room
Fred, they've taken the baby. I don't know.
My legs in stirrups.

No, this does not happen. *Does not happen anymore.*

I was on a ladder just yesterday, painting our house gold, covering this family with light.
I was eating sandwiches and painting and standing on a ladder.

In the kitchen, the bleeding. The doctor said he didn't know. The heartbeat is strong, I can hear it
as the gurney moves along the hallway.
I hear feet running on wet sand.

Keep trying.

At least you have other children. That's lucky.
Listen.
A grieving mother is not lucky.
Listen.
I'll leave the garage light on all night if I want.

He showered, he shaved. They told us we had time.
He didn't know. Why labor started with blood, not water. With this breaking.

My maple-leaf room
breaking down, shredding down
my thighs.
I was on a ladder.
      My milk is going to come in, tomorrow.

My mother. My sister. Birthday party, chocolate cake, and the funeral.
Fred carries the casket from the car, by himself. Her pink sweater buttoned.
                  Not too high, not too tight.

We are almost running down the hallway, the gurney clicking on the floor. I
hear the heartbeat. *Help me breathe.* Just squeeze my hand, says the nurse. *No,
I need to breathe. I know how to do this. I know. I am.* Don't push, she says. Just
don't push, whatever you do. The doctor's not here yet. *I*

    am alone in this room.
    My legs in stirrups.
    A nurse comes in, drapes a sheet
    over me.

My children lean over the banister, waiting for news. The ladder up against
the back of the house. A sandwich on a plate in the refrigerator, which hums
quietly, doing its job.
    She was here. With us.

    How many children do you have?
    Go back. Try again. You can't stop yet.

I have three.
I have three children

please, bring her to me.

They swaddle babies tightly, to comfort them, to womb them. Her blanket
has blue and white stripes. My milk is coming.

>I hold her still, small feet.
>I will have to give her back.

>>>*Please, leave us.*

>Look at this beautiful girl.
>My girl, Shawnya Hope.

And then, finally, she breathes. They wrap her tightly in a blue-and-white blanket, bring her back to me. I have lost my voice, but whisper her name over and over. You're okay. I have burst all the blood vessels in my face, I have no voice, and still more pain, and the placenta is stuck, but I have this breathing body, this breathing girl, here on my warm belly.

Evangeline's Birth

for my sister Sharra

It's not that complicated
what we want. Just perfection

at least in this one moment.
So when you are in the hospital

bed and the baby begins to crown—
it's happening so fast

nurses rushing
midwife distracted—

you need them to listen
because this has to happen in water.

Your girl, this longed-for, dreamed-about
sea star in your own ocean

needs to be born in water,
to swim from amniotic sac

to warm bath, your own waves
welcoming her into the world.

And so you get up out of that bed
baby hanging low, your belly

a full, creamy moon
and you take a walk harder than any man

has ever walked—forget Armstrong,
forget Aldrin. You voodoo

yourself into that tub,
spread your legs and Evie

slips out into water.
No sharp slap of air, no rough hands

just the long slide
of your body for her to climb,

a quiet rising, and into
that nest between your breasts

where she takes her first,
perfect, breath.

The doctor touches my bare feet, quietly leaves the room. The nurses turn down the lights, tuck clean sheets around me. I pull the baby close against my body, breathe in the smell of birth on her head. She is in her first sleep, and I listen to her breathing, watch her chest rise and fall—yes, still rising, yes, still falling. We have crossed this ocean, somehow, found our way to this new shore. In a few hours it will be about milk, and baths, and crying, and singing, and teaching her to latch, and her sucking my pinky finger, and visitors, and everyone holding her. But tonight, we only have to breathe, and sleep. Tonight, we have only to breathe and sleep.

In the Birthing Tub, Afterwards

—after an Amanda Greavette painting

Look at the swollen squash
of my belly, no longer sleek and fat.

Look at the broken blood vessels
in my face, in my eyes.

Look at the torn door
between my legs, at my stitches

at the baby's left ear
folded the wrong way

her color not yet peaches
and cream, a trace of vernix

in the creases of her arms.
In these minutes we lie back

and we are not
beautiful, we are not lovely,

baby and mama. We've arrived
on your doorstep, late at night

after walking long through
a forest that was not easy or kind.

Look at the snow
on our shoulders.

Look at the way we are just
beginning to shine.

About the Project

After giving birth to my third child, and knowing it was going to be my last, I began collecting birth stories. Like most women, I had been hearing them for years—at baby group, at story time at the library, and in friends' living rooms. I started this project by asking a doula in Juneau, Shayna Rowher, to share her story. We agreed I would give Shayna her poem when it was finished and only publish it if she liked it. That collaboration went well, so I continued, collecting stories from other mothers. In the third year of the project I approached X'unei Twitchell and he agreed to give me his daughter's story; I was delighted to have a story from a father. Later that year I asked Stephanie and Wendy Perry for their story, and they agreed, offering me their notes and memories so I could construct this story from two mamas. With the book nearly finished, I woke one night and realized there was a story that needed to be in this book—the story of losing a child during birth. My mother-in-law, Sharon Wall, was willing to give me her story. I am so grateful for the gift of these stories. This book is by and for these mothers and fathers.

Notes

What Does a Fetal Heartbeat Sound Like: This is a found poem. I posted this question on Facebook one day, and these are the exact words of the parents who wrote back.

Do Not Look at a Lunar Eclipse: These traditions come from the Thai, Inuit, Hispanic, Navajo, and Chinese cultures.

Shaawatke'é's Birth: Lingít birth speech and English translation by X'unei Lance Twitchell.

In the Birthing Tub Afterwards: This is an ekphrastic poem based the painting by Amanda Greavette. The painting can be viewed at http://amandagreavette.blogspot.ca/p/paintings.html.

All the stories in this book are published with the parents' permission. The stories told in "Catching Babies" are true but the names of the doctors and patients have been omitted.

Biographical Note

Emily Wall is a Professor of English at the University of Alaska. She holds an MFA in poetry, and her poems have been published in journals across the US and Canada, most recently in *Prairie Schooner* and *Alaska Quarterly Review*. She has been nominated for a Pushcart Prize and her book, *Flame*, won the Minerva Rising chapbook prize. Her poem "This Forest" was chosen to be placed in Totem Bight State Park in Ketchikan, Alaska. She has published three books of poetry: *Flame*, *Liveaboard*, and *Freshly Rooted*. Emily lives on Douglas Island in Alaska, and she can be found online at www.emily-wall.com.